WORKBOOK

Living *in the* Excellence *of* Jesus!

Written by Cheryl Price, Ph.D.
Edited by Evangeline Carey

UMI (Urban Ministries, Inc.)
Chicago, Illinois

Publisher:
UMI (Urban Ministries, Inc.)
P.O. Box 436987
Chicago, Illinois 60643-6987
1-800-860-8642
www.urbanministries.com

First Edition
First Printing

ISBN-13: 978-1-934056-65-3
ISBN-10: 1-934056-65-0

Table of Contents

CHAPTER 1

TRUSTING GOD IN THE UNEXPECTED

BASED ON LUKE 1:26–45

KEY VERSE: *"Gabriel appeared to [Mary] and said, 'Greetings, favored woman! The Lord is with you'"* (Luke 1:28, NLT).

LESSON FOCUS: God sent the Savior of humanity, the Messiah Jesus, God's one and only Son, through a virgin. Her name was Mary. God favored Mary enough to trust her and her betrothed (fiance), Joseph—who was Jesus' legal father, but not His biological father—with such a precious seed. This favor of God was so unexpected. In addition, there were serious ramifications for Mary, being pregnant with this *Child of the Holy Spirit*, in her unmarried state. Both she and Joseph had to trust God in the unexpected.

DO YOU KNOW . . .?

To prepare for the lesson, study the following words and definitions (all are taken from Chapter 1—"Trusting God in the Unexpected").

ambiguous—confusing, vague, unclear, uncertain

barren—infertile, sterile

excellence—brilliance, distinction, fineness, superior

trust—confidence, conviction, dependence, faith, hope, reliance

UP FRONT AND PERSONAL DISCUSSION QUESTIONS

1. Think of a nursery rhyme that you know and write it below. What do you think was the original intent or meaning of the nursery rhyme, and how is it understood today?

_____

_____

_____

_____

_____

_____

_____

2. In our everyday life experiences, we use or say things that mean something different from their original meanings; however, today it has a new meaning or is obsolete. List three items as examples and share your thoughts with the class.

	Item	Original Meaning/Intent	Present Meaning or Obsolete
Example:	**Coca-Cola**	**Medicine**	**Soft Drink**
a.	_____	_____	_____
b.	_____	_____	_____
c.	_____	_____	_____

3. After reading the Up Front and Personal section, define the word *trust* in your own words.

_____

_____

_____

_____

_____

4. Now, give an example of what it means to trust.

_____

_____

_____

_____

_____

5. How does one trust God, whom he/she cannot see?

_____

_____

_____

_____

_____

6. When should one trust God? Why?

_____

_____

_____

_____

7. How can you find or see the excellence of God in a situation that is characterized by both trauma and drama?

_____

_____

_____

_____

_____

A WORD FROM THE LORD

1. Review the background information on Joseph, Mary, Zechariah, and Elizabeth. Then fill in the blanks below with the names of some of your family members or close friends who are like family. Next, write three to four one-word descriptions about each person. Share with your class or small groups a funny or special story about a family member or friend that you listed.

Family Member   Description

_____   _____

_____   _____

_____   _____

_____   _____

2. Mary's pregnancy, before the marriage ceremony was completed, would have caused her to be ostracized and possibly stoned to death. Do you think the customs then were fair to teenage mothers or teenage fathers? Think of some of the various ways churches have responded to teenage pregnancies? How do your church and society overall respond today to teenage pregnancies?

_____

_____

_____

_____

_____

_____

3. Elizabeth was an older woman and was thought to be cursed by God because she was barren. The stigma of being childless in their culture was very great. What is your understanding of how society and your particular family respond to women and men who are "childless"?

_____

_____

_____

_____

_____

4. God always makes excellent choices as to who will carry out the Lord's work. Why do you think God chose Mary, a teenager, to be the mother of Jesus, and Joseph to be the legal father? If you were between the ages of 13–16, would God have been able to choose you to be the mother or father of Jesus? Why or why not?

_____

_____

_____

_____

5. Explain what Luke 1:26–45 teaches about "trust."

_____

_____

_____

_____

6. List some negative consequences of *not* trusting in God.

_____

_____

_____

_____

7. Paraphrase (state in your own words) and then personalize the following Scriptures on trust.

a. Job 13:15, paraphrased: _____

_____

_____

Personalized: _____

_____

_____

b. Psalm 18:2, paraphrased: _____

_____

_____

Personalized: _____

_____

_____

c. Proverbs 3:5, paraphrased: _____

_____

_____

Personalized: _____

_____

_____

d. Isaiah 50:10, paraphrased: _____

_____

_____

Personalized: _____

_____

_____

SOMETHING TO THINK ABOUT. . .

God's announcement, through the angel Gabriel, of Mary's conception is good news for Christians. To paraphrase an age-old question, is something good because it is good or because God said it is good? Explain your answer and give supportive information.

_____

_____

_____

_____

_____

A DOER OF THE WORD

1. When you look over your life now—your character (inward thoughts/feelings and outward expressions/actions), your relationship with Jesus and the church, your family, paid job/career choice, and your volunteer service—do you think you are living out, in all or some ways, what God originally meant for you to be and do? Why or why not? What can you do to make changes? Should you make changes?

_____

_____

_____

_____

_____

_____

2. What was the last crisis, or problem, that you faced? How did you work through the situation or how are you working through it? In addition to prayer, what other advice can you offer someone who is in a crisis?

_____

_____

_____

_____

_____

3. List two major crisis areas in the African American community. Then share how your church works with other churches and community groups to address these issues.

_____

_____

_____

_____

4. Name at least one person who has provided you with assistance and/or affirmation during a difficult time in your life. Then describe how you have assisted or given care to someone who was in a crisis or difficult situation. How did you feel during both of these experiences?

_____

_____

_____

_____

_____

PRAYER FORUM
Write a prayer or words of inspiration for someone who has been impacted by a personal or natural disaster.

_____

_____

_____

_____

_____

_____

_____

CHAPTER 2

IF THESE WALLS COULD TALK
(AND I BET THEY WOULD SAY SOMETHING, TOO!)

BASED ON JOSHUA 2:1–9, 12, 14–15

KEY VERSE: *"So the [two spies] set out and came to the house of a prostitute named Rahab and stayed there that night"* (Joshua 2:1, NLT).

LESSON FOCUS: Why would the two spies stop at the house of Rahab, who was a known prostitute? Was it because it was an ideal place for a quick escape in case they were discovered by the authorities? Or was it because it was a good place to gather important information, and certainly they needed to know all about their enemies? Or could it be that an all-knowing, all-seeing God directed them to go to Rahab's house because God had a plan for the salvation of humanity, and He was going to include Rahab in the lineage of Jesus Christ, the Savior? If these walls could talk, they would indeed have a story to tell.

DO YOU KNOW . . .?

To prepare for the lesson, study the following words and definitions (all are taken from Chapter 2— "If These Walls Could Talk").

community of faith—the collection of believers, the church

faith—assurance, confidence, conviction, reliance, trust

institutionalized slavery—businesses and other institutions have built-in rules and regulations that help them discriminate against or bypass certain racial and ethnic groups in hiring, job promotions, etc.

pandemic—catastrophic events that destroy many lives (HIV/AIDS, storms, tornadoes, etc.)

sin—a willful breaking of God's laws or rules

UP FRONT AND PERSONAL DISCUSSION QUESTIONS

1. Discuss how you think you would feel (or would have felt) if you were taking a trip to the slave castles.

_____

_____

_____

_____

2. Name seven countries in Africa and describe something you know about each of them.

a. _____

b. _____

c. _____

d. _____

e. _____

f. _____

g. _____

3. What sites in Africa would you like to visit and why? Is there any history that you want to share about your particular destination?

_____

_____

_____

_____

_____

_____

4. Name three slave revolt leaders. Do you think you would have escaped or assisted with the escape?

a. _____

_____

b. _____

_____

c. _____

_____

5. After reading the Up Front and Personal section, define the word *faith* in your own words.

_____

_____

_____

_____

_____

6. Now, give an example of what it means to have faith in God in the midst of great suffering.

_____

_____

_____

_____

_____

_____

7. How can you find or see the excellence of God in the Up Front and Personal account of the slave castles? Where was God in all that suffering?

_____

_____

_____

_____

_____

_____

_____

A WORD FROM THE LORD

1. What are some of the characteristics of Rahab and the spies that we can use in our lives to help deliver us in our problems?

_____

_____

_____

_____

2. List three assessments of Joshua and his leadership skills.

   a. _____

   _____

   b. _____

   _____

   c. _____

   _____

3. Who are the strong leaders in your church and why?

_____

_____

_____

_____

_____

4. Name two attributes that make a great leader.

   a. _____

   _____

   b. _____

   _____

5. We all must follow someone at some point in our lives. Do you agree or disagree? Are you a leader or a follower? If you are considered a leader or a follower by others, what makes you either one or both?

_____

_____

_____

_____

6. Explain how you will implement at least three practical applications from this lesson into your life.

_____

_____

_____

_____

_____

7. Paraphrase (state in your own words) and personalize the following Scriptures on faith.
   a. Matthew 9:22, paraphrased: _____

_____

_____

   Personalized: _____

_____

_____

   b. Luke 12:28, paraphrased: _____

_____

_____

   Personalized: _____

_____

_____

   c. John 3:16, paraphrased: _____

_____

_____

   Personalized: _____

_____

_____

SOMETHING TO THINK ABOUT. . .

1. Name two of the important persons listed in this section. Describe how you think their accomplishments have impacted the African American community and the world at-large.

_____

_____

_____

_____

_____

2. Discuss the effects of drug abuse within the African American population and its impact within our country. What are the responses to the drug problem from your church's perspective, and is this response enough?

_____

_____

_____

_____

_____

_____

_____

3. Why is the jail rate for African Americans so high, and what are the social and cultural implications for this epidemic? Share how you personally and your church collectively address the prison population problem for African Americans.

_____

_____

_____

_____

_____

_____

_____

A DOER OF THE WORD

1. Although we may not choose certain people to do particular duties for the Lord, discuss the reasons you think God chooses people that we would consider the outcasts of society.

_____

_____

_____

_____

_____

2. How effective is prayer without action in making changes to bring about a positive and healthy community for African Americans? What are some actions, in addition to prayer, that African Americans need to build a better community?

_____

_____

_____

_____

_____

_____

3. What are some of the destructive forces within the African American community? What are some of the positive forces?

_____

_____

_____

_____

_____

_____

PRAYER FORUM
Write a prayer or words of inspiration that address destructive fear in our lives.

_____

_____

_____

_____

_____

_____

_____

CHAPTER 3

WHEN GOD SAYS, "YES"!

BASED ON ACTS 12:5–17
KEY VERSE: *"Suddenly, there was a bright light in the cell, and an angel of the Lord stood before Peter. The angel tapped him on the side to awaken him and said, 'Quick! Get up!' And the chains fell off his wrists"* (Acts 12:7, NLT).

LESSON FOCUS: When we take our requests before our loving Heavenly Father, we should go expecting Him to answer. We should go pregnant with hope to Almighty God to meet our daily needs. In today's Scriptures, when the church prayed for Peter, while he was in prison, God answered their prayers so quickly that it caught Peter and them by surprise. Needless to say, they were not expecting Him to say, "yes." This was shown by their surprise at finding Peter delivered and standing at the door. When we go to God with our earnest petitions, do we expect Him to say, "yes"?

DO YOU KNOW. . . ?
To prepare for the lesson, study the following words and definitions (all are taken from Chapter 3—"When God Says, 'Yes'!").

a willing heart—an obedient heart to God's will and commands

an angel of the Lord—a messenger sent by God

giving God the victory—giving God the praises and glory for what He has done in our lives, is doing, and will do, based on His Word

God's favor—God's unmerited mercy and blessings upon our lives

Paul—the apostle who once persecuted the church, met Jesus on the Damascus Road, got saved, witnessed for Him by helping to establish many churches, and wrote many letters to these infant churches when they were in trouble; his letters make up much of the New Testament

the Last Supper—the dinner that Jesus had with His disciples in the Upper Room before His crucifixion

the Passover meal—the meal the Jews had in celebration of the time in Egypt when Jesus spared their firstborns from death and killed all of the Egyptians' firstborn because Pharaoh would not set the Israelites free from more than 400 years of slavery

to pray very earnestly—with trust, to sincerely petition God for our needs

UP FRONT AND PERSONAL DISCUSSION QUESTIONS
1. Anticipation and expectation can make us feel anxious and worried about whatever problems we are working on or working through. Share a time when you were waiting for a blessing and/or a breakthrough?

_____

_____

_____

_____

_____

_____

_____

2. Is your nature more like D. King's or Debbie's? Why?

_____

_____

_____

_____

3. Briefly describe your reactions and listening level when someone else is waiting on a blessing or breakthrough.

_____

_____

_____

4. List three Scriptures to help you and others work through their anticipations and anxieties while they are waiting to hear from God.

a. _____

b. _____

c. _____

5. When was the last time you gave up on God blessing you as you worked through your breakthrough? Why did you give up, and what was your response after "God showed up"?

_____

_____

_____

_____

_____

_____

A WORD FROM THE LORD

1. Describe the Jewish celebration of Passover and share how Passover is or is not celebrated within Christianity.

_____

_____

_____

_____

_____

2. Why should Christians celebrate or not celebrate Passover?

_____

_____

3. Are there any celebrations that are similar to Passover within the African American church? List and explain.

_____

_____

_____

_____

4. Share what you know about the disciple Peter.

_____

_____

_____

_____

_____

5. Do you have "Peter" qualities? If so, which ones?

_____

_____

_____

_____

_____

6. Is it a benefit or a blessing for you and for building the kingdom of God on Earth to have some of Peter's qualities?

_____

_____

_____

_____

_____

7. Why do you think John Mark's mother's home was the gathering place for the prayer service? Would your home be thought of as a place of prayer? Why? Why not?

_____

_____

_____

_____

_____

_____

8. Paraphrase (state in your own words) and then personalize the following Scriptures on prayer.
   a. Matthew 26:41, paraphrased: _____

_____

_____

   Personalized: _____

_____

_____

   b. Luke 11:1, paraphrased: _____

_____

_____

   Personalized: _____

_____

_____

   c. Romans 8:26, paraphrased: _____

_____

_____

   Personalized: _____

_____

_____

   d. Philippians 4:6, paraphrased: _____

_____

_____

   Personalized: _____

_____

_____

SOMETHING TO THINK ABOUT. . .

   1. Waiting on God's response requires patience on our part. How do you help yourself be patient with God? How do you help others develop a more patient attitude with God?

_____

_____

_____

_____

2. Why do you think Jesus did not heal everyone or assist everyone with a need? What are the ways that your church responds to the various needs within the church, the community, and the world? What are some of the ministries that your church can focus on and do for others with your assistance?

_____

_____

_____

_____

3. Does your church have a Watch Night Service? What are the reasons and the rituals your church celebrates Watch Night Service?

_____

_____

4. Are there different rituals that you would like to include in the Watch Night Service?

_____

_____

_____

_____

A DOER OF THE WORD
1. What are some of the ways that your church uplifts the power of prayer? Explain.

_____

_____

_____

2. How can you practice not worrying and trusting God in your times of need?

_____

_____

_____

_____

3. Describe your prayer life in times of difficulty and in good times. How do you share your experiences to help others who are going through difficult times and to encourage those who are not struggling to pray even in the good times?

_____

_____
_____
_____

4. If there is a prison ministry in your church, what are the responsibilities and how can you assist?

_____
_____
_____
_____

PRAYER FORUM
Write a prayer or words of inspiration thanking God for all He's done for you.

_____
_____
_____
_____
_____
_____
_____
_____

CHAPTER 4

AFRAID, BUT NOT ALONE

BASED ON JUDGES 4:4–16

KEY VERSE: *"Then Deborah said to Barak, 'Get ready! This is the day the LORD will give you victory over Sisera, for the LORD is marching ahead of you.' So Barak led his 10,000 warriors down the slopes of Mount Tabor into battle"* (Judges 4:14, NLT).

LESSON FOCUS: Barak, Israel's military leader, whose name means "thunderbolt," had been given a mission by God through Deborah, a prophetess and judge. God wanted him to lead the battle against King Jabin, who was a major enemy of God's chosen people, the Israelites. A man named Sisera led King Jabin of Hazor's army. They had 900 chariots of iron. When this "mighty" soldier, Barak, looked at the battle strategies with human eyes, instead of the fact that an all-powerful God was going before him to prepare the way, he became afraid. Therefore, he would not go into battle without Deborah by his side. This lesson will focus on trusting in Almighty God (having faith) when our fears try to win the day.

DO YOU KNOW . . .?

To prepare for the lesson, study the following names, phrases, and definitions. Match the words to the phrases that describe them (all are taken from Chapter 4—"Afraid, But Not Alone").

1. Barak
2. Deborah
3. Heber
4. Kedesh
5. King Jabin
6. Lappidoth
7. Naphtali
8. Sisera
9. the palm of Deborah
10. the Kishon River

a. commander of King Jabin's army
b. one of the 12 tribes of Israel
c. where Deborah lured Sisera and his troops
d. where Judge Deborah held court
e. commander of Israel's army
f. where Barak called together the tribes of Zebulun and Naphtali
g. prophetess and judge of Israel
h. a descendant of Hobab, Moses' brother-in-law
i. Deborah's husband
j. the king of Hazor, Israel's enemy

UP FRONT AND PERSONAL DISCUSSION QUESTIONS

1. Is there one or a few family members who have the responsibility to care for your family in various ways? Are you comfortable with this? Does it need to be changed? What can you do to make changes to this system?

_____

_____

_____

_____

_____

2. Share a time when you or someone in your family had to make a major sacrifice for your family.

_____

_____

_____

_____

_____

_____

_____

_____

_____

_____

3. When feeling excluded, family members have ways to hold other members emotionally hostage for what they did to help someone else in the family. Share an account that you have witnessed or have heard about.

_____

_____

_____

_____

_____

_____

A WORD FROM THE LORD

1. Why would Barak depend on Deborah instead of God?

_____

_____

_____

_____

2. Imagine and share how Deborah felt when Barak did not want to trust God's Word to him and what Barak must have felt when he lacked the courage to go into battle without Deborah?

_____

_____

_____

_____

_____

_____

3. What can men learn from Barak about following the leadership of women?

_____

_____

_____

_____

_____

_____

_____

4. What can women learn from Deborah about leadership and communication with God?

_____

_____

_____

_____

_____

_____

5. What can we learn from the biblical account of Deborah and Barak about fighting in spiritual warfare?

_____

_____

_____

_____

_____

_____

_____

6. Paraphrase (state in your own words) and then personalize the following Scriptures on faith.

    a. Matthew 17:20, paraphrased: _____

_____

    Personalized: _____

_____

_____

    b. Luke 18:42, paraphrased: _____

_____

_____

    Personalized: _____

_____

_____

    c. Ephesians 6:16, paraphrased: _____

_____

    Personalized: _____

_____

_____

SOMETHING TO THINK ABOUT...

1. In biblical times, why do you think it was a disgrace for a soldier to be killed by a woman?

_____

_____

_____

_____

_____

_____

_____

2. In today's society, do you think that there is too much emphasis placed on boys and men being strong, and girls and women being weaker? Why or why not? Is it acceptable within our society for men to show fear greater than women or vice versa? Give examples to support your beliefs.

_____

_____

_____

_____

_____

_____

3. Discuss ways that we are to be humble before God, and why fear can be beneficial as well as detrimental.

_____

_____

_____

_____

_____

_____

A DOER OF THE WORD

1. Name two people whom you can depend on to give you support when you are afraid or feel alone.

a. _____

_____

b. _____

_____

2. Can others depend on you for support when they are feeling afraid or alone? Share how you show that you are dependable to those who need you in a crisis or just support them with your presence or kind words.

_____

_____

_____

_____

_____

_____

_____

PRAYER FORUM
Write a prayer or words of inspiration that address the impact of God helping you in your spiritual battles.

_____

_____

_____

_____

_____

_____

_____

_____

_____

_____

JESUS IN STRANGE PLACES

BASED ON LUKE 19:1–10
KEY VERSE: *"Jesus responded, 'Salvation has come to this home today, for this man has shown himself to be a true son of Abraham'"* (Luke 19:9, NLT).

LESSON FOCUS: This lesson focuses on God's agenda and His ability to seek and save the spiritually lost, no matter who they are or where they may be. He sent His one and only Son (Jesus) to save the lost—those who needed a Savior.

DO YOU KNOW . . .?
 To prepare for the lesson, fill in the blanks from the list below (all are taken from Chapter 5—"Jesus in Strange Places").

a. Abraham	d. notorious sinner
b. Jericho	e. sycamore
c. Man	f. tax collector

1. Jesus met Zacchaeus in the city of _____ (Luke 19:1).
2. Zacchaeus was a _____ (his occupation) (v. 2).
3. Zacchaeus climbed in a _____ tree to see Jesus (v. 4).
4. Zacchaeus was considered to be a _____ _____ by the rest of the Jews (v. 7).
5. Zacchaeus showed himself to be a son of _____ (v. 9).
6. Jesus, the Son of _____, came to seek and save the spiritually lost (v. 10).

UP FRONT AND PERSONAL DISCUSSION QUESTIONS
1. What is your definition of "spirituality" and "spiritual"?

_____

_____

_____

_____

_____

_____

2. Name some of the rituals that you practice to develop your spiritual life.

_____

_____

_____

_____

_____

3. Who has Jesus shown favor to that you are willing to admit you were either surprised about or did not think they deserved the blessing?

_____

_____

_____

_____

_____

4. When was the last time you wanted to see Jesus in your life with the enthusiasm of Zacchaeus?

_____

_____

_____

_____

5. Share the time when you truly felt sorry for your sin, so you gave back to others or gave extra special blessings to others.

_____

_____

_____

_____

_____

_____

6. Why is society often cruel to those who are considered "odd" or "imperfect"?

_____

_____

_____

_____

_____

_____

7. Why do you think that God chooses "imperfect" people as vessels He can use to help build His kingdom?

_____

_____

_____

_____

_____

_____

A WORD FROM THE LORD

1. Name two individuals that represent Zacchaeus in your life and what makes them like Zacchaeus.

   a. _____

   b. _____

2. From what you have read about Zacchaeus, did the other Jews have a right to hate him so much? Why?

   _____
   _____
   _____
   _____

3. When is being a tax collector a noble profession?

   _____
   _____
   _____
   _____
   _____

4. In your own words, why was Zacchaeus so desperate to see Jesus?

   _____
   _____
   _____
   _____
   _____

5. Did Zacchaeus have a right to see Jesus? Why?

   _____
   _____
   _____
   _____
   _____

6. Did the rest of the Jews really know who Jesus was and His purpose for coming into this world? Explain.

   _____
   _____

7. Paraphrase (state in your own words) and then personalize the following Scriptures on faith.

   a. 1 Chronicles 17:18, paraphrased: _____

_____

_____

   Personalized: _____

_____

   b. Psalm 69:5, paraphrased: _____

_____

_____

   Personalized: _____ _____

_____

_____

   c. Psalm 139:1–2, paraphrased: _____

_____

_____

   Personalized: _____

_____

_____

SOMETHING TO THINK ABOUT. . .

1. What is bullying?

_____

_____

_____

_____

2. Do you see any differences between bullying today and when you were growing up?

_____

_____

_____

_____

3. Share your thoughts on why the Good Samaritan and the woman who gave all her money did their best. What can we learn from them about a Christian's understanding of helping others who are in need regardless of our circumstances?

_____

_____

_____

_____

4. What programs and people in your church represent the transformed Zacchaeus? How can these programs be enhanced to reach others, and what can church members learn from the people who have a Zacchaeus spirit?

_____

_____

_____

_____

_____

A DOER OF THE WORD

1. Describe a time that you were picked on or talked about someone (out loud or secretly) who was odd or different from the group. Maybe they did not agree with the group about an idea or dressed in a strange way. As a believer, what should you have done?

_____

_____

_____

_____

_____

2. Describe how your church deals with people who are different from the norm of the congregation.

_____

_____

3. Were you ever bullied in your life? How did you handle it? If you were a bully, why did you act this way?

_____

_____

_____

4. When people are bullied, they can believe that they are helpless victims. As believers, how should we respond to people who feel this way?

_____
_____
_____
_____

5. What would Jesus have us do to encourage living in His excellence and not in the shadows of the bullies at church, at work, in school, at home, etc.?

_____
_____
_____
_____

6. Explain how you will implement at least three practical applications from this lesson into your life.

   a. _____

   b. _____

   c. _____

7. List the areas in your life that need to be nurtured and encouraged to grow as you work toward the excellence that God has placed within you. If you do not have areas in your life that are underdeveloped, how are you helping someone else to be the best that he/she can be (but not as your clone)?

_____
_____
_____

PRAYER FORUM
Write a prayer or words of inspiration that ask for help in the areas in your life that need changing so that you can be all that God is calling for you to be.

_____
_____
_____
_____
_____
_____
_____

CHAPTER 6

A KNEE-BENT HEALING

BASED ON MARK 5:25–34

KEY VERSE: *"For [the sick woman] thought to herself, 'If I can just touch his robe, I will be healed'"* (Mark 5:28, NLT).

LESSON FOCUS: Life sometimes deals us a desperate hand. After all, even though this fallen world is not our permanent home, we are still in the world. Plus, believers are in spiritual warfare. Ephesians 6:10–12 (NLT) instructs us to, "Be strong in the Lord and in his mighty power. Put on all of God's armor so that you will be able to stand firm against all strategies and tricks of the devil. For we are not fighting against flesh-and-blood enemies, but against evil rulers and authorities of the unseen world, against mighty powers in this dark world, and against evil spirits in the heavenly places." Therefore, just because we are believers, we are not immune from the problems of life. We, too, get sick, have lean financial times, need encouragement, and face trials and tribulations that no one but God can bring us through. These dilemmas can drive us to our knees before Almighty God. Such was the case with the woman in today's study. She needed a higher power to do what man could not do.

DO YOU KNOW . . .?

To prepare for the lesson, study the following facts (all are further study for Chapter 6—"A Knee-Bent Healing").

- The disease that the woman had seemed incurable.
- The condition caused the woman to bleed constantly.
- It made her ritually unclean, excluding her from most social contact.
- The woman was desperate!
- Under Jewish law, if she touched Jesus, it would have made him unclean as well.
- The woman was considerate of Jesus. She reached out and touched His robe instead.
- The woman's faith caused her to be healed.

UP FRONT AND PERSONAL DISCUSSION QUESTIONS

1. When sickness becomes a part of your family, name four ways that they respond. If you are the primary caretakers or one of them, what are your responsibilities, and how has this changed your life?

_____

_____

_____

_____

_____

_____

2. Know that sickness may lead to death, no matter how hard we pray. Are you prepared to deal with the financial, emotional, and spiritual issues that come with sickness and death? (Having a will, insurance, or money—or access to money—for a funeral and the burial should already be in place.) If so, how are you prepared? If not, why not?

_____

_____

_____

_____

_____

_____

3. Staying healthy is important for a variety of reasons. How do you maintain your health?

_____

_____

_____

_____

_____

4. If you know someone who has cancer, has had a heart attack, or has any other debilitating illness, how have you ministered to him/her or his/her family? If you have not, how can you minister?

_____

_____

_____

_____

_____

_____

A WORD FROM THE LORD
1. What type of disease do you think the woman had?

_____

_____

_____

_____

2. Discuss what emotions probably ran through the woman as she touched the hem of Jesus' robe.

_____

_____

_____

_____

3. Since she was isolated from society, how do you think the woman felt? Why?

_____

_____

_____

_____

_____

4. Did the disciples ask a valid question when they asked Jesus why He had asked them who touched Him, being that there was such a large crowd? Why or why not?

_____

_____

_____

_____

_____

5. Have you ever questioned Jesus? Share. What was His response to you? If you have not questioned Him, why not?

_____

_____

_____

_____

_____

6. Paraphrase (state in your own words) and then personalize the following Scriptures on faith.
    a. Psalm 7:1, paraphrased: _____

_____

_____

Personalized: _____

_____

_____

    b. Isaiah 12:2, paraphrased: _____

_____

_____

Personalized: _____

c. Matthew 12:21, paraphrased: _____
_____
_____

Personalized: _____
_____
_____

SOMETHING TO THINK ABOUT...

1. Diseased, desperate, and delivered was the woman who was healed. She was an outcast and considered unclean by her community. Who are the unclean or the ignored members of your family, church, or neighborhood?

_____
_____
_____
_____
_____
_____
_____

2. Is their status self-imposed and/or imposed by others? Explain.

_____
_____
_____
_____
_____

3. Do you help to make a difference in their lives? If so, how?

_____
_____
_____
_____
_____

A DOER OF THE WORD

1. To promote healthier eating and living, encourage all church groups to serve only healthy snacks and meals at church and leave out the red punch and red drinks. Discuss why you think the artificial preservatives and dyes in these drinks would be a concern for your health.

_____

_____

_____

_____

_____

2. List the foods you have eaten over the last few days.

_____

_____

_____

_____

_____

3. Would Jesus want to eat with you, and would He feel that you were eating a healthy meal? Why or why not?

_____

_____

_____

_____

_____

4. If He came to your house or church for a meal or a snack, would you serve Jesus the food you ate? Why or why not?

_____

_____

_____

_____

_____

_____

PRAYER FORUM

Write a prayer or words of inspiration asking God to help you make good decisions when choosing what foods to put in your body.

_____

_____

_____

_____

_____

_____

_____

_____

_____

_____

CHAPTER 7

AN EXPENSIVE MEAL

BASED ON DANIEL 1:5–12

KEY VERSE: *"But Daniel was determined not to defile himself by eating the food and wine given to them by the king. He asked the chief of staff for permission not to eat these unacceptable foods"* (Daniel 1:8, NLT).

LESSON FOCUS: There are critical choices in life that believers have to make. We have to choose daily to obey and honor a Holy (set apart from sin) God. By our daily living, we must choose to reverence and bring glory to His name. When Daniel was taken away into captivity to Babylon as a young man, he and the three young assistants chose to honor God at all costs. The king's food and lifestyle were too expensive for them to indulge. We will explore how they walked with the Lord in a foreign land, when even their lives were at stake. God kept them and met their needs in the trouble. I pray that what we learn will inspire us to reach for excellence in serving our God, because indeed He is the Good Shepherd.

DO YOU KNOW . . .?

To prepare for the lesson, study the following facts (all are further study from Chapter 7—"An Expensive Meal").

- Even while Daniel and the three assistants were in bondage in Babylon for 70 years, a Sovereign God was still in control of world events.
- God is in control of His universe and never out of control.
- An all-powerful God will overcome evil with His good.
- Daniel and the three assistants were positive role models of dedication and commitment to a Holy God.
- We do not have to compromise our faith, even in a hostile environment.

UP FRONT AND PERSONAL DISCUSSION QUESTIONS

1. The "Genesis" family knew how to love and share what they had with others. How does your church and biological families share love with others?

_____

_____

_____

_____

_____

_____

_____

_____

_____

_____

2. Write a news article that describes how you would have rewritten the ending of this story.

_____
_____
_____
_____
_____
_____
_____
_____

3. Describe your favorite family event from your childhood or from today. Think about how you laughed or ate your favorite food or listened to the "family history."

_____
_____
_____
_____
_____
_____

4. Share your tradition for holidays or any other special time.

_____
_____
_____
_____
_____
_____
_____

A WORD FROM THE LORD
1. Why was Daniel able to stay focused and committed to his diet?

_____
_____
_____
_____

_____

_____

_____

_____

2. If you struggle/have struggled with food or any other form of addiction, how do you/did you stay focused on how not to participate in whatever it was that could harm you?

_____

_____

_____

_____

_____

_____

3. Write and speak the names of the young Hebrew men before they were changed. Should we honor their translated Hebrew names or only say the "new" names given to them? Why? Why not?

_____

_____

_____

_____

_____

_____

_____

4. God often sends a "ram in the bush" to help us when we are held prisoner in various ways. Daniel and the other men had a "ram in the bush." Who was he and who has been your "ram in the bush"? Explain.

_____

_____

_____

_____

_____

5. Paraphrase (state in your own words) and then personalize the following Scriptures on faith.

a. Mark 2:5, paraphrased: _____

_____

_____

Personalized: _____

_____

_____

b. Romans 2:7, paraphrased: _____

_____

_____

Personalized: _____

_____

_____

c. 1 Timothy 6:11, paraphrased: _____

_____

_____

Personalized: _____

_____

_____

SOMETHING TO THINK ABOUT. . .

1. Who are the people you most admire for taking a stand for justice and why?

_____

_____

_____

_____

_____

_____

2. Describe a time you took a stand for justice.

_____

_____

_____

_____

_____

_____

_____

3. What were the results, and who helped you in your quest for justice?

_____

_____

_____

_____

_____

_____

_____

A DOER OF THE WORD

1. Fasting and prayer are two ways to prepare ourselves for service for the Lord. Select one food or drink item that you will give up for 30 days. Also, select a behavior or thought you will not give in to for 30 days. Feel free to keep a journal in words or pictures to share about your 30-day journey. When will you begin your fast?

_____

_____

_____

_____

_____

_____

_____

_____

_____

_____

2. Designate a particular time of day to pray for strength to sustain you and your classmates. You may want to select a prayer partner during the next 30 days. You can check on and pray for each other once a week or every day.

_____

_____

_____

_____

_____

_____

_____

PRAYER FORUM

Write a prayer or words of inspiration asking God to help you walk in His principles and honor Him, even when life seems impossible.

_____

_____

_____

_____

_____

_____

_____

_____

_____

_____

_____

_____

CHAPTER 8

TROUBLE IN THE CAMP

BASED ON JOSHUA 6:16–21; 7:1, 10–13, 20–21

KEY VERSE: *"But Israel violated the instructions about the things set apart for the LORD. A man named Achan had stolen some of these dedicated things, so the LORD was very angry with the Israelites. Achan was the son of Carmi, a descendant of Zimri son of Zerah, of the tribe of Judah"* (Joshua 7:1, NLT).

LESSON FOCUS: God desires obedience from those who are called by His name. Part of believers' worship of a Holy God is to obey His commands. This lesson focuses on the consequences of disobedience. God specifically spelled out how the battle of Jericho was to be fought to His chosen people (the Israelites). He was leading in the fight and was going to bring the victory. He gave the Israelites the charge to obey His edicts to the letter. Therefore, when Achan chose to disobey, Achan brought trouble into the Israelites' camp. The consequences were death to him and his entire family. We, too, bring trouble into our own lives as well as those of others when we disobey an all-knowing, all-present, and all-powerful God. Others are either blessed or suffer because of the choices we make. Clearly, we should choose to obey God.

DO YOU KNOW . . .?

To prepare for the lesson, study the following names, phrases, and definitions. Match the words to the phrases that describe them (all are taken from Chapter 8—"Trouble in the Camp.")

1. Achan	a. possessions that God deemed should be set aside for Him
2. Joshua	b. a monument commemorating the killing of Achan and his family
3. Rahab	c. disloyal, disobedient
4. sacred	d. thief, disobedient to God's commands
5. "the Lord's treasury"	e. the prostitute in Jericho, who helped the two spies sent by Joshua to spy out the land
6. "the Valley of Trouble"	f. set apart for God
7. unfaithful	g. Moses successor, led the Children of Israel into the Promised Land (Canaan)

UP FRONT AND PERSONAL DISCUSSION QUESTIONS

1. Write your ending to the Marcus story and how you think the family reacted to his death.

_____

_____

_____

_____

_____

_____

2. What was your initial thought as to what made Marcus slightly different?

_____

_____

_____

_____

3. After examining your own family, share some thoughts on the different personalities and roles that each person plays. Where do you fit in and how do you see yourself?

_____

_____

_____

_____

4. Name three positive characteristics about your family as a whole.

a. _____

b. _____

c. _____

A WORD FROM THE LORD

1. Why do you think Achan wanted to steal the treasures that were to be dedicated to the Lord's house?

_____

_____

_____

_____

2. Do you think in Achan's case, the punishment fit the crime? Why or why not?

_____

_____

_____

_____

3. If someone from your family commits a crime, do you think the entire family should pay? Give examples to support your belief.

_____

_____

_____

_____

_____

4. Do you think crime or godly ways would be different if the entire family had to pay very stiff penalties (i.e., monetary fines, shame, jail time) for one member's criminal behavior or ungodly behavior in the church?

_____

_____

_____

_____

_____

5. What is your definition of "godly" or "ungodly" behavior?

_____

_____

_____

_____

_____

6. What were the repercussions that you experienced when doing what the Lord did not want you to do?

_____

_____

_____

_____

_____

7. What were the treasures that Achan stole and why were they important to the Lord's treasury?

_____

_____

_____

_____

8. Discuss why Joshua was an excellent leader.

_____

_____

_____

_____

9. What were some of the difficulties and rewards he faced as a leader of ex-slaves?

_____

_____

_____

_____

_____

10. Share your understanding of why the number seven is a number of significance within the Judea-Christian faith.

_____

_____

_____

_____

_____

11. Paraphrase (state in your own words) and then personalize the following Scriptures on faith.

a. Genesis 2:16–17, paraphrased: _____

_____

Personalized: _____

_____

b. Matthew 5:20, paraphrased: _____

_____

Personalized: _____

_____

c. 1 John 2:6, paraphrased: _____

_____

_____

Personalized: _____

_____

_____

SOMETHING TO THINK ABOUT. . .

1. Achan stole from the treasury of the Lord. Are Christians ever guilty of stealing from the Lord? Explain.

_____

_____

_____

2. Name three ways that you think Christians steal from the Lord.

_____

_____

_____

_____

3. List different ways that maybe you need to give back to God on a daily basis.

_____

_____

_____

_____

_____

A DOER OF THE WORD

1. List three social programs that your church is actively participating in financially and with people and/or supply power.

a. _____

_____

b. _____

_____

c. _____

_____

2. Do you think Jesus wants us involved with passing laws and regulations to help provide better health care for all Americans? Why or why not?

_____

_____

_____

_____

3. If you believe that justice should impact all aspects of our lives, how do you see Christians as change agents in your particular community and in the world?

_____

_____

_____

_____

_____

_____

4. What are you doing personally and collectively to make justice a major focus in your life and the lives of others?

_____

_____

_____

_____

PRAYER FORUM
Write a prayer or words of inspiration asking God to help you be obedient to His Word so that you can walk in the excellence of God.

_____

_____

_____

_____

_____

_____

_____

_____

_____

CHAPTER 9
WORKING HARD OR HARDLY WORKING?

BASED ON NEHEMIAH 1:3–4; 4:1–9; 5:15–16

KEY VERSE: *"At last the wall was completed to half its height around the entire city, for the people had worked with enthusiasm"* (Nehemiah 4:6, NLT).

LESSON FOCUS: Our focus is on the call of God. God wants vessels He can use to be workers to help repair the broken temples and walls of people's wasted lives. He wants workers to go to the highways and byways and be witnesses for Him—to help build His kingdom. Even though Nehemiah was a common man, exiled in a foreign land, and serving as a cupbearer to the Persian king Artaxerxes, he was still not out of God's reach. In fact, a Sovereign God (one who is in control and never out of control) called Nehemiah to return to Jerusalem, his home, and rebuild the temple and walls that lay in waste from the time their capturers destroyed them and took many of their young men into captivity, including Daniel. Nehemiah shows us today how to walk in excellence before a Holy God because God called him and he answered.

DO YOU KNOW. . . ?

To prepare for the lesson, study the following facts (all are further study for Chapter 9—"Working Hard or Hardly Working?").

- As an exile in a foreign land, Nehemiah was subject to King Artaxerxes.
- Even though the Israelites had been in bondage to the Babylonians for approximately 70 years, Jerusalem's walls were still in ruin from the battle.
- Nehemiah was to lead the third expedition of freed Israelites back to their homeland.
- Nehemiah was not only a man of character, but one of persistence and prayer, even in a foreign land.
- Because of Nehemiah's dedication, persistence, and prayer, the wall was built in 52 days.
- Even in captivity, Nehemiah did not give up on His God.

UP FRONT AND PERSONAL DISCUSSION QUESTIONS

1. Share memories you may personally have or someone you know may have in experiencing racism, sexism, etc.

_____

_____

_____

_____

_____

_____

2. What are some of the benefits for those who marched in various protest marches during the 1950s through 2000s (war protests included)?

_____

_____

_____

_____

_____

_____

_____

_____

3. Name one or two people today who have made valuable contributions to your life. Share what they have done that you are grateful for.

_____

_____

_____

_____

_____

_____

_____

4. Now write a "thank-you" note to the two people who have blessed you so much.

_____

_____

_____

_____

_____

_____

_____

A WORD FROM THE LORD
1. What are some of the character traits that Nehemiah possessed that helped him to stay strong in the work of the Lord even under extreme opposition?

_____

_____

_____

_____

2. Why did the leaders not want Nehemiah and the other workers to complete the building of the wall?

_____

_____

_____

_____

_____

3. What is your response to naysayers in the church or for progressive movement for justice in the community or the church?

_____

_____

_____

_____

_____

_____

_____

4. Recount a time when you were opposed to being supportive of someone who wanted to do something that you thought should not be done (i.e., helping someone else in their time of need), but he/she made the best choice.

_____

_____

_____

_____

_____

_____

_____

_____

5. How did you respond during and after the completion of the task recounted in number 4?

_____

_____

_____

_____

6. Paraphrase (state in your own words) and then personalize the following Scriptures on faith.
   a. Matthew 9:37–38, paraphrased: _____

_____

_____

Personalized: _____

_____

_____

b. Luke 10:3, paraphrased: _____

_____

_____

Personalized: _____

_____

_____

c. John 21:15, paraphrased: _____

_____

_____

Personalized: _____

_____

_____

SOMETHING TO THINK ABOUT. . .

1. Nehemiah took a stand to build the wall in spite of the taunts and teasing from others. His faith, hard work, and the contributions of others paid off and the wall was built. Think about a time that you gave up before you finished a project and a time when you stayed with a project regardless of what others said and it paid off. Share.

_____

_____

_____

_____

_____

2. Describe why you gave up and why you hung in there.

_____

_____

_____

_____

_____

_____

_____

3. What Scriptures, songs, or people come to mind that gave you a sense of strength and the hope to keep trying?

_____

_____

_____

_____

_____

A DOER OF THE WORD

1. When is faith an obstacle and when is it a blessing? (You can define the word *faith* as having faith in God or faith in whatever you want to.)

_____

_____

_____

_____

_____

_____

_____

_____

2. List programs and/or relationships that you built in your lifetime that others have supported or worked against. Why did others support or not support your work?

_____

_____

_____

_____

_____

_____

_____

3. Write out a covenant with the Lord on giving excellent service and work to a particular project that you desire to complete. Include a time limit.

_____

_____

_____

_____

_____

_____

_____

PRAYER FORUM

Write a prayer or words of inspiration asking God to help you be in tune to His call upon your life and move you to excellence in your worship of Him.

_____

_____

_____

_____

_____

_____

_____

_____

_____

_____

_____

_____

_____

CHAPTER 10

ROI: A RETURN ON INVESTMENT

BASED ON MATTHEW 25:14–26, 28

KEY VERSE: *"The servant to whom he had entrusted the five bags of silver came forward with five more and said, 'Master, you gave me five bags of silver to invest, and I have earned five more.' 'The master was full of praise. "Well done, my good and faithful servant. You have been faithful in handling this small amount, so now I will give you many more responsibilities. Let's celebrate together!"'"* (Matthew 25:20–21, NLT).

LESSON FOCUS: The investments that God has made in us are very important to Him. Our focus this session will be on using our time and talents wisely and to Almighty God's glory. Therefore, we need to go to Him in prayer and find out what His will is for our lives and pursue walking in His will. In order to achieve excellence in our worship of a very deserving God, we must let Him lead us into bringing an excellent return on what He has entrusted to us.

DO YOU KNOW. . . ?

To prepare for the lesson, study the following words and definitions (all are taken from Chapter 10—"ROI: A Return on Investment").

entrusted—a possession given in the care of someone else

faithful servant—one who uses his/her talent(s) and time wisely (to the glory of God)

lazy servant—one who does not use his/her talent(s) and time wisely (to the glory of God)

ROI: A Return on Investment—the profit after all the expenses are paid

servant—one who serves; God considers all believers servants to Him and humanity

the kingdom of God—presently it reigns in all believers' hearts because we have accepted Jesus Christ as our Lord and personal Savior; all believers will reign with Jesus on the new Earth that is to come

the rich master—the rich master in the story represents God

UP FRONT AND PERSONAL DISCUSSION QUESTIONS

1. Describe a time when you thought your own accomplishments were due to your efforts and no one else's.

_____

_____

_____

_____

_____

_____

2. Is the thinking in number one good or hurtful? Why or why not?

_____

_____
_____
_____
_____

3. Do you know of anyone who believes that pulling him/herself up by his/her own bootstraps is realistic? Share.

_____
_____
_____
_____

4. What would be another word or phrase to use in place of boots and bootstraps when discussing self-help?

_____

5. Discuss what it means to work together individually and collectively for the Lord and if both or one way is better than the other. Give examples to support your beliefs.

_____
_____
_____
_____
_____
_____
_____
_____
_____

A WORD FROM THE LORD
1. Explain how this story makes you feel about the Master (God)?

_____
_____
_____
_____
_____
_____

2. Reread the explanation of the servant who was given the one talent as to why he did not invest the money. Discuss his response and how it applied then and does or does not apply today?

_____
_____

_____
_____
_____
_____

3. What do you think the servant, who did not invest, is saying in regards to his actions?

_____
_____
_____
_____

4. Do you think that the first two servants wanted to invest the money so they could be free and have their own investment firms, or freedom to do what they wanted? Why or why not?

_____
_____
_____

5. Paraphrase (state in your own words) and personalize the following Scriptures on working for God.
   a. John 15:1–2, paraphrased: _____

_____

   Personalized: _____

_____

   b. John 15:4, paraphrased: _____

_____

   Personalized: _____

_____

   c. John 15:7, paraphrased: _____

_____

   Personalized: _____

_____

_____

SOMETHING TO THINK ABOUT. . .

1. Jesus has a way of asking questions that address the real problem in our lives? How would you respond to Jesus' question, "Do you want to be healed?" What do you need to be healed from today?

_____

_____

_____

_____

_____

2. Is education the key to success at all times? What forms of education do we need to have to be successful in life? Explain.

_____

_____

_____

_____

_____

3. Is Carter G. Woodson's "back door mentality" of control true today? Why? Why not?

_____

_____

_____

_____

_____

4. Discuss ways to change the back door mentality way of thinking and living.

_____

_____

_____

_____

A DOER OF THE WORD

1. Describe the after-school programs in your church. Who is responsible for the program? Are science and math a part of these programs?

_____

_____

_____

_____

2. Do you think that math and science are a part of the Scriptures? Share your reasons why or why not. Use Scriptures to support your answer.

_____

_____

_____

_____

3. What does the word *education* mean to you? How important is education to you, your family, and your church? Share how important you think education is to the African American people.

_____

_____

_____

_____

PRAYER FORUM
Write a prayer or words of inspiration asking God for help in bringing in a good return on His investment in you.

_____

_____

_____

_____

_____

_____

_____

NOTES

conf# MC 11/30
9821846

877 880 7001 Fax
Attn: Michael Himes
(216) 212-6124
Cleveland, Ohio

7400 Temple Hills Road
Camp Springs, Md. 20748

Debt Aire
800 916 4939

257
Dec 1: Doris Draughn
Lindsay cadillac (503)6478640
Dr. Marshall